100 KEYS

TO

PREVENTING AND FIXING WOODWORKING MISTAKES

Alan and Gill Bridgewater

BETTERWAY BOOKS

A QUARTO BOOK

Copyright © 1996
Quarto Inc.

First Published in
the U.S.A. by
Betterway Books,
an imprint of
F & W Publications, Inc.
1507 Dana Avenue
Cincinnati, Ohio 45207
(800) 289 0963

ISBN 1-55870-429-9

This book was
designed and produced
by Quarto Publishing plc
The Old Brewery
6 Blundell Street
London N7 9BH

Contents

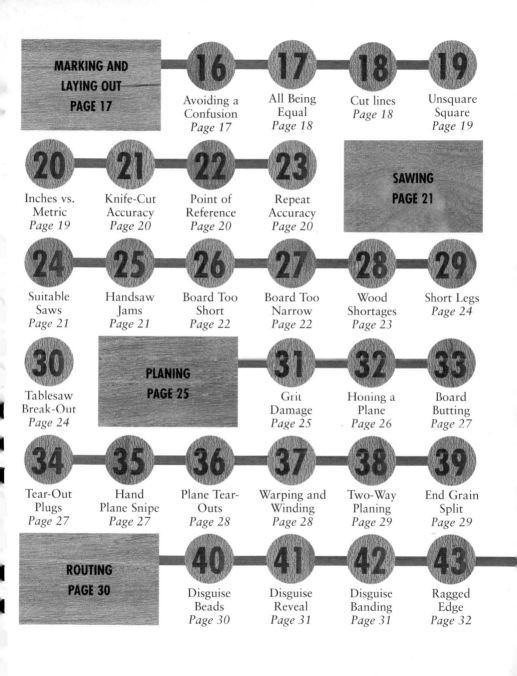

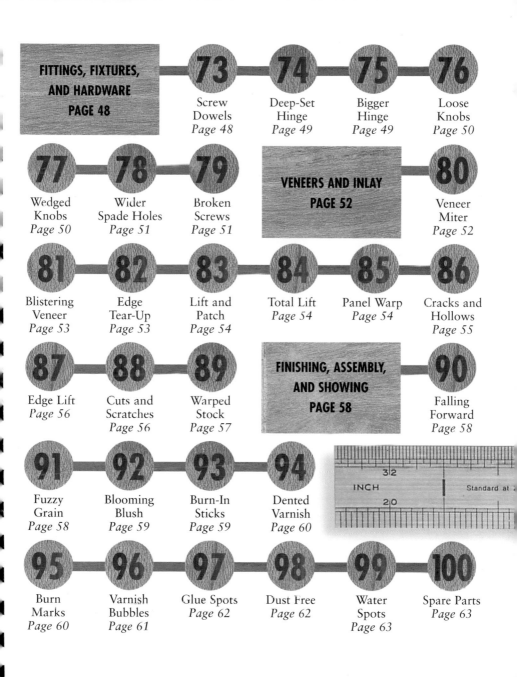

INTRODUCTION

I DON'T KNOW WHO SAID "If you haven't made a mistake then you haven't made anything," but I've got a feeling that he or she was a woodworker. Can't you just see yourself at the end of a project, showing your masterpiece to your family and buddies, and then justifying your all too obvious mistakes by coming out with such an adage?

Don't get too disheartened, you are not the first woodworker to make a mess-up, and you certainly won't be the last. Just about every woodworker who ever was has experienced that surge of angst, on discovering that their project has legs that are too short, or one of the joints is loose, or the newly veneered surface is developing a nice bunch of blisters. And then they had to figure out ways of making good. That's what woodwork is about. If you don't believe me, take a trip to a city museum and have a good, long, close-up look at all the furniture that has been made over the last four or five hundred years. Your museum studies will confirm that the woodworkers of the past were incredibly skilled at patching, scarfing, filling and making good. And don't think that all the repairs that you see on museum furniture are the result of restorations, not a bit of it. To my mind there is plenty of evidence to suggest that many of the repairs and design changes were made in answer to botch-ups that occurred when the items were first built.

In many ways I admire the qualities and skills that are needed to overcome woodworking blunders and mistakes more than I esteem the skills needed to build a faultless piece of furniture. To my way of thinking, the whole area of correcting woodworking mistakes is somehow Chaplinesque. It is about the little guy making good against all odds. I'm sure you know what I mean. It's about such positive traits as tenacity, perseverance and stubborn determination.

The wonderfully exciting thing about woodwork is that there are as many mistakes to be made as there are woodworkers to make them. Part of the fun and pain is the fact that mistakes seem to take on so many forms. It's almost as if new woodworkers spend time thinking up new problems. My tongue-in-cheek boast is that I never make the same mistake twice, but rather I'm always thinking up new ones!

This book offers you all manner of tips, maneuvers, strategies and keys for avoiding and correcting one hundred of the most common woodworking blunders. And even if you haven't made the specific mistakes as set out, then our overall strategy and approach will help you to develop your own unique way of overcoming your own woodworking problems.

We have designed the book so that it more or less follows the average making sequence of searching out the raw wood, initial preparations, marking out, sawing, planing and so on. Each tip, with its hands-on photograph or drawing, has been carefully thought through so that it sets out the extent of the mistake and then tells you how to avoid it or repair it.

So remember, we have all been there. Best of luck.

AVOIDING BASIC FLAWS IN WOOD AND PRIMARY DAMAGE LIMITATION

Though this book is mostly about fixing your hands-on-tool mistakes – meaning blunders and mishaps that you make in the woodshop – a whole heap of potential problems can be avoided at the point of purchase. The way you select your wood in the lumber yard; the type, figure and quality of the wood; and what you do to the raw wood when you first get it back to the workshop – all these factors have a bearing on the success of the project. The following tips will help you to side-step wood problems.

1

WHAT WOOD? Since the best way to fix a mistake is not to make it in the first place, you should always start each project by searching out suitable wood types. First, forget about color and figure. Just focus on points like strength, board width, traditional use and availability. For example, if you want to carve a plain wood toy for a toddler, you should look for a wood that is relatively easy to carve, a wood that is non-toxic, a wood that doesn't splinter, a tight-grained wood that doesn't leach out color, and so on. You would most likely go for traditional woods like beech or pine. You certainly wouldn't choose *yew*, which is poisonous, or *jelutong*, which is soft grained and fragile. Don't make the mistake of choosing the wrong wood.

Michael Thonet's 19th century bentwood chair designs in beech demonstrate how important it is to choose the right species for a job.

2

QUALITY CONTROL Avoid wood that looks in any way to be overly knotty, warped, split or wet. If you have any doubts at all about a log or board that you have already purchased, saw a thin slice from one end and check it over for problem cracks and soft areas. If the sample crumbles, then you can't lose if you repeatedly re-run the procedure until you come to sound wood.

Saw off a slice and check it for problems. Rerun the procedure until you come to sound wood.

SPECIES	COMMON APPLICATION	VISUAL QUALITIES	STRENGTH	FLEXIBILITY	AVAILABILITY
OAK	joinery	varied	good	high	good
ASH	chair making	bold	good	medium	medium
ELM	chair seats	rich	good	high	poor
BEECH	joinery	bland	good	medium	medium
CHERRY	decorative	rich	medium	medium	good
POPLAR	general	bland	good	low	medium
MAPLE	general	clean	good	high	good
PINE	general	varied	medium	low	good
WALNUT	cabinets	rich	medium	medium	medium
LIME	carving	silky	poor	low	medium

3 **LOOSE KNOTS** Although it's pretty annoying when a loose knot falls out, and you are left with a hole, there are two sure-fire ways of fixing it. The easiest is to smear a generous amount of epoxy on all mating faces and tap the knot back in place. But if, say, the loose knot crumbles, you can plug the hole with a whittled peg. All you do is whittle the peg from a piece of matched wood, glue and plug the hole from the best face. After the glue is set, trim and plane the plug down flush with the surface.

Drill out the knot hole and make good with a glued plug.

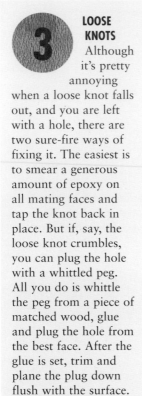

1. Appraise the extent of the crack – its length and depth.

2. Cut a butterfly key to size and shape.

3. The key needs to be two thirds of the thickness of the slab.

4. Use a bevel edge chisel to chop out the mortise hole.

4 **LIMITING CRACKS** The best way of dealing with a large check or crack – say in one end of a massive slab tabletop – is not to try to conceal it, but rather to secure it with a decorative butterfly key. The double dovetail shape is cut from wood that is half the thickness of the tabletop. The mortise hole is cut with a chisel so that the "wings" of the butterfly bridge the crack. Be sure the grain direction of the butterfly is perpendicular to the wood it joins or the butterfly will have no strength. The key is glued and hammered in place. After the glue dries, the butterfly is planed flush with the surface.

RAISING A DENT A dent can be disastrous! Picture this: You have prepared a board, it's a real beauty, and BANG! you drop a hammer on the surface. The problem is, of course, that the small dent – be it ever so minute – will really show when the piece is finished. The good news is that the dent can easily be raised by steaming. The procedure is very neat: All you do is set a damp cloth on top of the dent and apply pressure with a hot household iron. Don't let the steam iron directly touch the wood. It's a good idea to first practice on the back of the board or some scrap wood just to make sure that your chosen wood type doesn't warp, stain or misbehave under such treatment.

Repeatedly steam the offending dent until it vanishes from view.

HALTING SPLITS Fine hairline splits that occur after joinery has been cut, meaning low-stress splits caused by uneven drying, can be quickly fixed by gluing and clamping. Ease as much glue as you can into the split. It helps to first thin the glue. As you apply it to the split, gently squeeze the board and then let go, so that capillary action will draw glue all the way into the split. When the split is fully coated with glue, clamp up, and wait for the glue to set. Then take a cabinet scraper and scrape the repair down to a good finish.

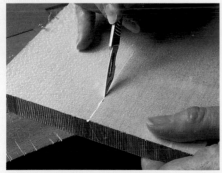

1. Use a scalpel to ease the glue into the split.

2. Wipe away excess glue and clamp up.

AVOIDING BASIC FLAWS IN WOOD AND PRIMARY DAMAGE LIMITATION

7 **STAINS** You need to take special care in choosing your wood. Always avoid wood that is in any way stained. If the dealer assures you that a stain is only skin deep, ask him if you can take a small sample home to plane and sand. A good tip is to wipe the sample over with a cloth dampened with mineral spirits or naptha. Any permanent stains will be revealed.

Typical stick-marked and water-stained wood.

8 **COLOR CHANGE** Wood by its very nature is always going to change color – when it is being converted and worked, and over its life time. But it sometimes happens that an unwanted streak of color shows itself. For example, cherry wood sometimes reveals an unexpected dash of fluorescent white-yellow sapwood. In this instance, you can either bleach the whole works and then restain, or better yet, you can think of the yellow as being a positive feature that needs to be built and book-matched into the design.

PREPARATION AND SECONDARY DAMAGE REPAIR

O kay, so you have chosen your wood with great care and caution: It is of a size and type to suit your needs. Now you are eager to select the various boards for your next project. Not only is this the stage when you need to look long and hard at the quality of the raw lumber, it's also a time when you can steer around problems and make good some of the mistakes that occurred during storage, seasoning and transport.

9 WANEY EDGE One of the biggest mistakes raw beginners make when selecting thick, roughsawn boards, is that they measure the waney boards across their greatest width, rather than across their narrowest. They optimistically forget that the angled bark-covered edge – the waney area – is going to be wasted. Just remember, all the waney edges will need to be removed before you can square-up the boards.

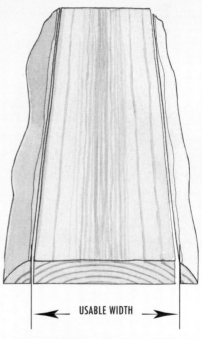

← USABLE WIDTH →

Be mindful that waney edges need to be wasted, and mark off the usable width of the wood accordingly.

Cut away the waney edges so as to achieve a usable board width.

10 **INSECT DAMAGE** Occasionally, you will come across a piece of wood that is perfect in every respect, apart from the fact that it is pierced through and through by a number of insect holes. The best procedure is to knife-cut a number of dowels from the same stock, flood the holes with super glue (cyanoacrylate), and then follow up by driving the dowels in after the glue. This done, you simply knock off the dowel ends and plane the wood to a good finish. If you can do this when the wood is in the roughsawn stage, then so much the better.

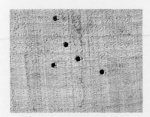

1. Assess the size of the bore holes and whittle dowel pegs to fit.

2. Flood the holes with glue and drive the dowels home.

3. When the glue is set, cut the surface down to a smooth finish.

11 **REDUCING WASTE** Having said that a waney-edged board will have to be cut back, don't make the mistake of always cutting the board length back to a single end-to-end straight edge. For example, if the board is wide, and the edge is excessively wavy, and you are looking to convert the wood into short pieces, then it might be possible to get an extra piece or two from the "waves." It might pay you to fit and fiddle around, laying out boards for the best use of the sound wood.

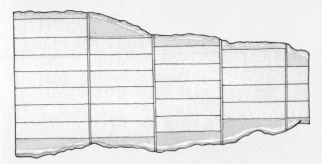

If you require a number of short length repeats, then spend time setting out the wood for the most efficient cut.

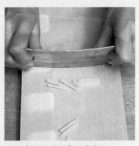

1. Run the scraper diagonally across the grain.

2. For best effect, vary the angle of cut and the flex of the scraper.

3. Tidy up the finish by skimming parallel to the grain.

12 **SCRAPING DOWN** If a flaw is more than a dent that can be easily raised and less than a gash that needs to be plugged, then often the best way forward is not to use a plane and/or sandpaper to level the wood. Instead, use a cabinet scraper to skim the surrounding wood down so that the blemish vanishes from view. In action, the scraper is first angled so that it runs diagonally across the grain and then runs parallel with the grain. It won't dig into the flaw like the plane, and it leaves a smoother finish than the sandpaper.

13 **HYDRAULIC GLUING** Here's the scenario: You have planed a board to a beautiful finish, and you notice a split running about 2 inches into the end grain. The problem is how to introduce glue into the split without smearing it over the face of the wood. The answer is delightfully direct. All you do is first drill a ¼-inch diameter hole down into the end of the board, into the end grain, so that it follows the course of the split. Next, stick clear plastic tape over the split at each side of the board. Then pour epoxy glue down into the hole, and finally follow it up with a push-fit dowel. The piston action of the dowel will force the liquid glue into the fissures.

Drive the push-fit dowel down in after the glue.

14 VOIDS IN WOOD Of course, if you saw into a slab of, say, oak, and find a massive swirling cavity, this isn't a mistake as such. The mistake is then going on to use the wood in the wrong context. The best approach is not to try to fill or plug the void, but rather to save the wood for a decorative project like a small table top or a sculpture – a project that makes a feature of the void.

15 BLACK IRON STAINS A common mistake is to leave a rusty iron nail or tool on a damp board – damp oak is often particularly bad – with the effect that the wood is stained blue-black. The foolproof method of removing such stains is to mix up a thick solution of oxalic acid and water, and flood the surface of the wood. Next day, you can brush up the dry crystals, wash the area with clean water, and the stain will have vanished.

1. Even the smallest iron stain can ruin a fine finish.

2. Flood the stained area with oxalic acid solution and leave it until the water has evaporated.

3. The stain has vanished – magic!

MARKING AND LAYING OUT

Just about every woodworker you are likely to meet will sooner or later come up with the musty old woodworking adage "measure twice and cut once." Certainly it is a bit wearisome to hear the same bit of woodshop folklore repeated ad infinitum, but then again, it's absolutely right. The fact of the matter is that huge numbers of mistakes can be avoided or remedied at the measuring and marking-out stage, before you ever get to cutting the wood.

16 AVOIDING A CONFUSION As a lot of mistakes have to do with mixing up the various faces of the wood, it follows that it's a good idea to identify the parts with pencil marks. The method shown – with marks and numbers – not only identifies the "face side" and "face edge" of a small panel, it shows the order of edge planing. The neat idea is that if you start by taking off the back edge corners with a chisel, and then plane the edges in the numbered sequence, you will avoid corner splitting.

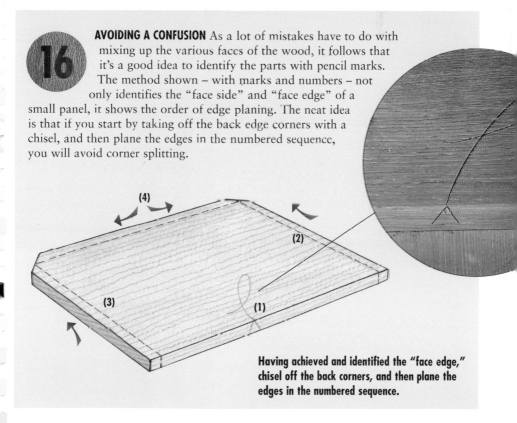

Having achieved and identified the "face edge," chisel off the back corners, and then plane the edges in the numbered sequence.

17

ALL BEING EQUAL When raw beginners to woodwork are faced with the challenge of how to divide an odd width board into a number of equal widths, they often make the mistake of trying to solve the mind-bending problem with a calculator and/or long division arithmetic. Let's take it that your board is at a non-standard measurement – say somewhere between 2–15 inches wide – and you want to divide it into four equal widths. The delightfully easy solution is to set a ruler or yardstick at a sloping angle across the board so that 0 inches is on one edge and 16 inches is on the other. Mark it off at 4, 8 and 12 inches, and then run parallel lines along the board. Easy, isn't it?

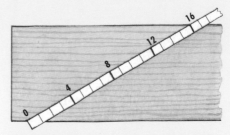

1. Set the ruler across the board and mark off four equal divisions.

2. Run parallel lines through the marked-off points.

18

CUT LINES A classic mistake is to make a cut on the wrong side of a drawn line, with the effect that the resultant joint is a bad fit. The best procedure is to lay out the shape of the joint first with a knife, ruler and square. Then check the measurements and the position of the joint against your working drawings. Next shade in the areas that need to be cut away, and finally make a point of running the line of cut to the waste side of the drawn line – meaning on the shaded area. Be mindful that the saw kerf must be entirely in the waste wood. Otherwise the thickness of the saw blade will be added to your measurements.

19 UNSQUARE SQUARE

It's plain to see that if your try-square is at fault, then all your laying out is going to be less than perfect. To test that the square is indeed set to a right angle, first set it down on a length of straight-edged lumber so that the stock is butted hard up against the edge. Then draw a line along the steel edge. This done, flip the square over, keeping it butted to the same edge, and run a second line over the first. If you can't get the two lines to match-up, then you need to get yourself another square. If you have a choice, go for an adjustable engineer's square.

1. Set the square against the stock and draw a line.

2. Flip the square over and attempt to draw a second line over the first.

20 INCHES vs. METRIC

Currently in Europe and America there is something of a measurement miasma, with book and magazine publishers variously opting to use a mish-mash of metric and inches. Woodworkers can be more than a little confused. What invariably happens is that the woodworker, in an attempt to work both systems hand-in-hand, makes a measurement slip-up that results in the workpiece being cut to the wrong size. Best advice is not to try to work both systems in the same harness. Better to spend time prior to the project converting all the measurements to one or the other – either all inches or all metric, whichever you are most comfortable with.

KNIFE-CUT ACCURACY When you are running marks across a board, it's very easy to make a mistake simply by marking the line with a fat pencil. The problem is that if you cut to the waste side of a fat, blurred pencil line, then your measurements could be out by $\frac{1}{16}$ inch or more. And, of course, if you mark out all your stock with the same fat pencil, then the mistake will be compounded. The best procedure is to check and double-check the measurement requirements and then to accurately and delicately score the line with a knife. Get rid of that blunt pencil!

POINT OF REFERENCE A frequent mistake made when marking out a joint with the square and mortise gauge, is forgetting to always limit your point of reference to the prepared good face and good edge. This potentially disastrous mistake can very easily be avoided, simply by making sure that you pencil-label the "face side" and "face edge" as soon as they have been achieved.

REPEAT ACCURACY Mistakes often occur when two or more pieces have to be identically marked. What usually happens is that small inaccuracies creep in at both ends of all pieces, with the effect that all lengths and joints are a poor match. To avoid this mistake, simply clamp the members together and square the marks across. For still closer accuracy when hand-sawing, you can set the blade down on the mark and then slide the square so that it is hard up against the blade.

1. Clamp all the members together so that the joint shoulders are aligned.

2. For super accuracy, set the knife point down on the mark and slide the square up to the blade.

SAWING

There's no doubt about it – sawing is the time when projects are made or broken. Certainly the act of sawing is pretty dynamic, and it's not so easy to correct a bad sawing mistake, but then again, the right saw cut, in the right place at the right time, can positively transform a project. The following tips will show you how to make every kerf count.

SUITABLE SAWS One of the biggest mistakes you can make is choosing to cut your stock with the wrong type of saw. This holds true whether you are using a big power saw or a simple handsaw. If you are just starting out, a basic selection of handsaws can tackle everything you need to cut. Choose a crosscut saw for crosscutting, a coarser-toothed ripsaw for ripping (cutting with the grain), a fine-toothed backsaw for cutting moist joinery, and a coping saw for curves and really fine work. A table saw is the woodshop power tool workhorse, but make sure it's saddled with the right blade for the job. Carbide-tipped blades hold their edge longer. A combination blade will handle most cross-cutting and joinery tasks. A coarser rip blade takes that duty. Fine-tooth blades are great for cutting plywood without splintering. For resawing large stock, trade the table saw for a bandsaw.

HANDSAW JAMS If you want to avoid the very annoying problem of handsaw jams and slips, and/or it is essential that the ends of your workpiece be sawn perfectly square, it's a good idea to run the marking knife or chisel at a sloping angle hard up against the waste side of the try-square, so as to cut a channel in which the saw can run. This will also help to eliminate tear-out and is especially useful when cutting joinery.

For sawing precision, use a knife to score the line of cut.

BOARD TOO SHORT One of the most bothersome blunders is to design a project to suit a limited number of carefully selected boards, only to find that one or other of the boards is easily wide enough but ever-so-slightly short. The great news is that you can save the work simply by slicing the board from corner to corner, so that you have two triangles. Then slide the two halves along so as to increase the length, being careful to match grain as best you can. Finally glue the sliced halves back together.

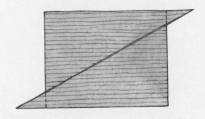

1. Saw across the diagonals.

2. Realign the two pieces so as to achieve a greater width.

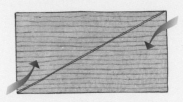

BOARD TOO NARROW If you find that one of your carefully selected boards has plenty of length but is a little bit too narrow, you can saw it across the corners and offset and butt glue the two halves in much the same way as described in the previous tip. Only this time, of course, you slide the boards along in the other direction so as to increase the width and decrease the length. If the board is to be used in a situation where strength is critical, reinforce the butt-glued joint with dowels or biscuits.

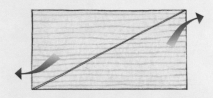

1. Saw across the diagonals.

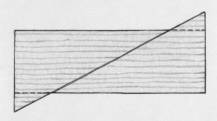

2. Realign the two pieces to achieve a greater length.

28

WOOD SHORTAGES If you make the classic mistake of optimistically estimating your matched stock and then find at the end of the day that you just don't have enough wood, then you may be able to make up what you need by splitting and laminating. The technique is wonderfully quick and easy. All you do is resaw the board (through its thickness) and glue common stock to your special wood. Then plane down to the required thickness. This technique is especially useful when the back is hidden from view – as with table tops, aprons, skirtings, plinths and the like.

1. Use the band saw to slice the choice wood down into thick "veneers."

2. Glue the choice wood at either side of the common stock.

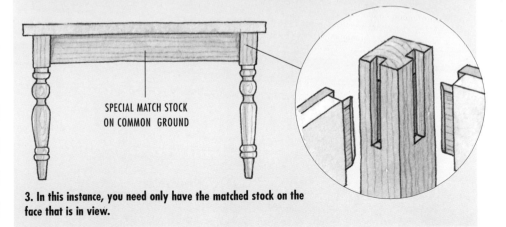

SPECIAL MATCH STOCK
ON COMMON GROUND

3. In this instance, you need only have the matched stock on the face that is in view.

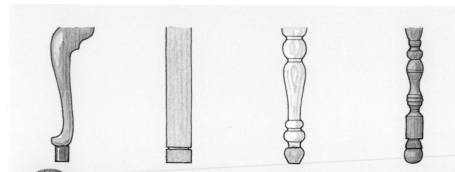

29 **SHORT LEGS** If you make the truly horrible mistake of sawing the legs on a table an inch or so too short, you will be faced with the problem of how to add a few inches to the legs – how to add feet – without making a total mess of the design. The best solution is not to try to hide joints with paint or a splice – it is rarely successful – but rather to side-step the fact that a mistake was ever made by ensuring that the added shoes, or castors, or turned buns, or blocks, or whatever, look to be a positive design feature. Use dynamic shape and wood color to draw the eye away from the seams.

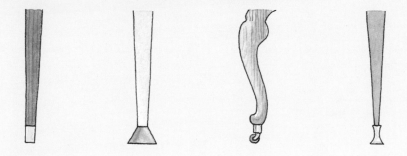

30 **TABLESAW BREAK-OUT** Crosscutting wood on table saws will normally result in slight splintering – known as break-out – on the underside. The problem is more acute when cutting veneered boards and plywood. Break-out can be avoided by inserting a sheet of hardboard underneath the workpiece and cutting through both layers at the same time. The hardboard supports the vulnerable cross-grain edge and contains the break-out.

PLANING

The act of planing is almost magical. One moment you have a raw rough-cut surface, and then next you have a smooth, flat surface that glows with color, figure and reflected light – a surface that is just asking to be touched. It is the planed surface that is the promise of things to come. Certainly planing is a procedure that is fraught with possible mistakes, but we show you a few tasty tips that will help you make the grade.

31 **GRIT DAMAGE** Grit and planes are a really bad mix! What happens is that heavy boards and timbers are often repeatedly dropped on their ends when they are transported from the mill to the lumber yard, and the lumber yard to the workshop. That means that the end grain is compacted with dirt and grit. And of course, when the wood gets to be planed in your shop, the grit not only makes a mess-up of all the cutting edges, it also scratches the wood. The best quick-fix is to routinely saw off a 1-inch-thick slice from the gritty ends before the stock is ever brought into the workshop.

Remove grit and paint.

Saw off the plank end before you start machining.

32

HONING A PLANE Most hand planes don't come from the factory ready to use. The bevel may be ground on the plane iron, but it isn't really sharp until it has been properly honed. A whole treatise could be written about sharpening – and has been! – but we'll give you a quick lesson here: Buy a selection of whetstones ranging from coarse to fine. If you buy oil stones, you'll need to use honing oil to lubricate the stones. If you use water stones, ordinary water will do. Honing angle is critical, and it takes practice to keep a plane iron at the right angle when sharpening by hand. Save some effort and buy an inexpensive honing aid that holds the blade at the correct angle on the stone. Run the blade over each stone, going from coarse to fine, until you have a razor sharp edge.

Smoothing plane

Oil stone

Water stone

SET AT ANGLE AND DRAG

1. Set the primary bevel down on the stone, raise the blade so that the cutting bevel is in contact, and then draw the blade towards you.

2. Remove the "wire" by gently wiping the back of the blade flat-down on the stone.

BOARD BUTTING A very common mistake, when jointing the edge of a long board that is going to be crosscut in half and then glued together edge-to-edge to make a wider board, is to finish up with an edge that is canted over at an angle. If this happens, don't go to all the aggravation of jointing the edge again. Turn one or other of the boards around so that the angled edges butt together to cancel out the error.

 TEAR-OUT PLUGS If, when you are jointing the edge of a length of wild-grained stock, a section lifts and tears, then the best remedy is to fit a boat-shaped plug – sometimes called a diamond "dutchman." The procedure is to remove the edge tear-out by making two angled saw cuts, cut a plug from matching stock, and then glue and clamp, and plane to a good finish. The secret of success is to use a fine-bladed saw and to be very careful that the two angled cuts meet without crossing.

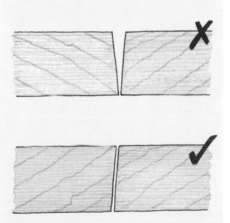

Match the grain of the plug and glue in place.

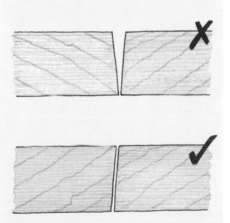 **HAND PLANE SNIPE** Many beginners to handplaning find that they repeatedly finish up with boards that are "sniped" or thinner at start and finish. This problem or mistake is easily corrected simply by pushing down on the knob at the forward end of the plane at the beginning of the stroke, and pushing down on the handle at the back end of the plane at the end of the stroke. Or, put another way, imagine that you are trying to plane a hollow, and adjust your pressure and stroke accordingly.

27

36 **PLANE TEAR-OUTS** If your typical metal hand plane digs into the board you are planing, there are a number of possible solutions. The simplest and most likely is that you have the blade or plane iron adjusted for too much depth of cut. If that's not the case, check that the chip-breaker, the part screwed to the back of the plane iron, is as close to the cutting edge as possible, and that there is no daylight between them when you sight through from the side. If your plane has a lateral adjustment, make sure it is set so the blade is perfectly parallel with the sole of the plane. A third possibility is that the frog, the triangular cast iron part that the plane iron and chip-breaker assembly rests on, is set too far back. Move it forward so it fully supports the plane iron, and so that the mouth of the plane is as small as possible.

37 **WARPING AND WINDING** If you are presented with a short board or panel that has warped or twisted along its length, then you will have to figure out a way of removing the wind. If the problem is with a small board – say the side of a cabinet – then the easiest solution is to use a hand plane to reduce the high corners. Having first used a couple of winding sticks to determine the severity of the wind and the position of the high spots, work the plane diagonally across the wood – from high spot to high spot – until the front face of the board is true.

1. Sight across the winding sticks. If they are slightly off parallel – as shown – then the surface is dipped.

2. Plane off the high spots and then rerun the sighting procedure.

1. The blade is set too far back – not enough depth.

2. The blade is set too far forward – too much depth.

3. Sight along the plane and set the blade bevel parallel with the sole.

TWO-WAY PLANING If you are a beginner to hand planing and have made the mistake of trying to through-plane a piece of wood that has a wild changing grain, then you will no doubt be presented with a board that has an area of torn grain. The sure fix is to first set the plane blade so that it takes the finest of skimming cuts. Clarify how the grain runs and then make good by planing in one direction and then the other.

END GRAIN SPLIT If the wood begins to split off when you are planing end grain – say on a panel – then you will have to first make a repair and then change your technique. The repair is simple enough; all you do is ease epoxy into the split, as already described, and clamp up. When the glue is set, pack out the end of the run with a block of scrap wood, clamp the block firmly in place, and then plane as before. If the workpiece is small, then you could use a block plane.

1. If you plane across end grain, you risk splitting off the wood.

2. A sacrificial waster clamped hard up against the workpiece takes the brunt of the split-off.

ROUTING

The traditional woodworking technique of cutting a groove or rabbet in one board, a mating tongue or rabbet in another, and then fitting the two boards together, is one of the oldest and best ways of making a strong wood joint. That said, the traditional methods of cutting the various rabbets, grooves and tongues – with hand planes and chisels – has been almost completely eliminated by the development of the electric router. Though few modern tools have had such a dynamic impact as the router – its decorative and joinery potential are truly enormous – it also has to be said that router mistakes tend to be big and bothersome. If you have just acquired a power router and are busy making one or two of those blunders, then the following tips will show you how to ease the aggravation.

40 **DISGUISE BEADS** If you have made a botched joint at some point along the line – say a really bad glued joint that is on full view – then you might be able to conceal the mistake by routing a decorative bead. Depending upon the character of the workpiece, you might go for a pretend tongue-and-groove bead, or a simple V-groove reveal. Of course, if the bad joint is important structurally to the piece, disguising won't be enough.

1. This ragged joint is an ugly sight.

2. The V-groove draws the eye away from the bad fit and finish.

DISGUISE REVEAL If you have made the classic mistake of building a table with an apron that is too narrow – to the extent that the tabletop needs to be lifted by about 1 inch – you can make good by routing a deep shadow trench or a bead-and-reveal. The procedure is first to glue a 1-inch-high strip of matching wood along the top of the apron, and then run the router along the strip so as to create a decorative bead molding and shadow trench along the joint line.

DISGUISE BANDING To disguise a badly glued and clamped seam, a shallow groove can be routed to fit a length of decorative inlay banding. Being mindful that bandings vary in width and thickness, it's always a wise idea to search out the banding before you start routing the groove.

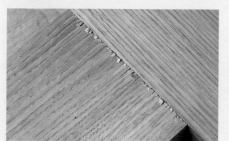

1. A badly glued and clamped seam.

2. Rout a trench to fit a strip of inlay banding.

3. Glue the inlay in the trench and strap it in place with masking tape.

43 **RAGGED EDGE** If you have made the mistake of trying to butt-joint two boards end to end, or you have a sawn end on a carcase – meaning one that runs out at the edge of the frame – you will almost certainly be presented with an unpleasant ragged edge. If this is the case, then it can be made good by routing a chamfer, or a reveal, or a V-groove that runs across the torn fibers.

1. An unpleasant ragged edge needs fixing.

2. A V-groove routed across the torn fibers is a good way of making an unsightly mistake into a feature!

44 **PANEL TEAR-OUT** A very dangerous mistake made when routing is to swing your body around the router to the extent that you suddenly find yourself pulling rather than pushing. If this happens, the router bit invariably snags into end grain and does damage to one side of the panel. If you have made such a mistake, the best way of repairing it is first to saw off the damaged side of the panel and plane back to a straight, true edge. Then glue on an extra strip to make up the width, and finally re-run the router.

1. Be warned – if you find yourself pulling rather than pushing, then you are heading for problems!

1. A classic router goof.

2. Make good by running a more generous profile run over the mistake.

PROFILE MESS-UP The scenario is: You are a beginner, and you have run a router profile around the edge of a panel, and it looks a mess – generally a bit thin, mean, and ragged. The question is – what to do? The simple answer is that you can't lose if you fit a larger bit in the router and run a second more generous profile over the first.

2. An ugly router "bite" needs fixing.

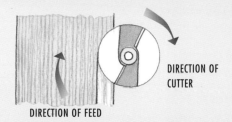

3. Saw off the damage, glue on a strip to make up the loss, and then take another run with the router.

DIRECTION OF CUTTER

DIRECTION OF FEED

Note the direction of spin and direction of feed.

Follower bearings should be regularly checked for wear.

JIG MISTAKE A great many router mistakes have to do with the jig being badly designed and/or inadequate. When designing a jig, it is best to have guide rails at both sides – to fit the base of the router. You will find that such an arrangement nicely counteracts the clockwise spin of the bit.

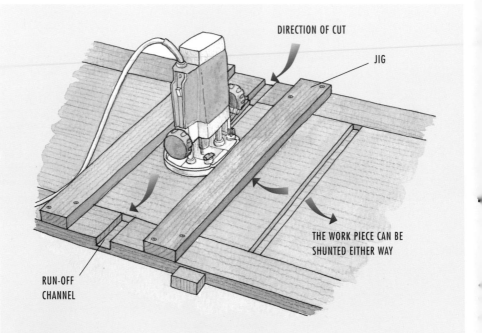

DIRECTION OF CUT

JIG

THE WORK PIECE CAN BE
SHUNTED EITHER WAY

RUN-OFF
CHANNEL

 JIG RUN-OUT A lot of mistakes have to do with sloppy practices. For example, many beginners to routing make the classic blunder of making contact with the workpiece before switching on the power or switching off the power before breaking contact. The best way of sorting this problem out – especially when you are plowing grooves and cutting housing channels – is to make a jig that completely frames the workpiece. In use, the router is switched on, lowered into the jig, run across the workpiece and into the other side of the jig, and then switched off and lifted out. Used in this way, the jig bears the brunt of your switch-on blunders rather than the workpiece.

CUTTING AND FIXING JOINTS

There are just about as many tools and techniques for cutting joints, and as many joints types to be cut, as there are woodworkers looking to cut them. Every joint is a joyous challenge, but every joint is also a potential minefield of mistakes. Who ever it was that said, "Every project is only one joint away from disaster," would certainly have drawn comfort from the following sure-fire ways of making good.

48 **LOOSE JOINTS** If you have made the miscalculation of cutting a joint too loose, then a quick repair is to pack the joint out with shavings. First, cut a number of wedges from shavings – with the grain running along the length of the shaving. Then, one at a time, dip the shavings in PVA glue and tap them home into the sloppy joint. Finally, trim back with a sharp knife and sand or scrape down to a good finish.

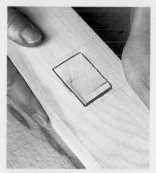

1. Assess the size of the mistake – the gaps.

2. Cut four thin wedges or shims to fit the gaps.

3. Dip the shims in glue and tap them home.

4. When the glue is dry, plane down to a good finish.

49 **LAMINATED TENON** A frequent error when making rails, is to reach the assembly stage – with the mortise-and-tenon joints all beautifully cut to a perfect fit – only to find that you have made the stupid mistake of cutting one or other of the rails about ½ inch too short. If this happens, you can fix it by taking three lengths of thinner stock and laminating a three-layer extension to fit the tenon. If you choose your wood with care, and plane back to a good finish, then you will achieve a good strong joint that will be nearly invisible.

1. Cut three identical lengths to fit the joint.

2. Glue and clamp in place.

3. Plane the extension down to a good finish.

50 **LOOSE DOVETAIL** If you have cut a dovetail to the wrong side of a draw line, the joint will be loose by the thickness of the drawn line – say about ¹⁄₁₆ inch on both sides. The remedy is to glue strips of veneer to both sides of the tail, and then to trim to a tight fit and reglue.

1. Make up the thickness by gluing strips of veneer to the sides of the tails.

2. Glue and fit, and trim to a good finish.

51 BROKEN TENON A common mishap is to be cutting a delicate tenon, only to find that the wood has a hidden cavity or a twist in the grain that causes the tenon to break off, leaving you with a crisp shoulder and a ragged stump. If this happens, then the best thing to do is to trim the break back flush with the shoulder, and then cut a mortise in the end of the rail. Finally, cut and trim a loose tenon to fit both mortise holes, and glue it in place. Make sure the loose tenon isn't too long.

1. Mark across the diagonal and cut a slot.

DIAGONAL WEDGE A good way of fixing a badly cut through mortise and tenon joint – meaning a joint that is so loose and sloppy that it just won't hold together – is to use a diagonal wedge. Let's say that there is an all-around gap of about 1/16 inch. The procedure is to run a saw cut from corner-to-corner down the length of the tenon and trim a thin hardwood wedge to fit. Next, spread glue over both faces of the wedge and drive it in place in the diagonal kerf. Drive the wedge in until the spreading tenon fills the mortise.

LOOSE TENON

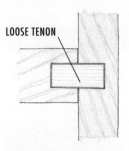

Glue the loose tenon in place and clamp up.

2. Tap a glued wedge down into the slot.

3. Trim the wedge to a good fit-and-finish.

53 **FOXTAIL WEDGE** If you have cut a loose-fitting blind tenon, the problem is how to fix it. You could pack the tenon out with veneers, but the best tried and tested technique is to use a clever little device called a foxtail wedge. First, cut a wide wedge kerf down the length of the tenon. Then a short fat wedge to fit, and finally glue and clamp. If you do it right, the fat end of the wedge will be driven hard up against the blind mortise, with the effect that the tenon spreads and holds.

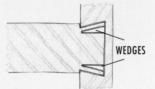

WEDGES

A double foxtail wedge.

54 **DOUBLE-WEDGE** If your through-mortise-and-tenon joint is tight across the cheeks but loose across the ends – so that the tenon slides lengthwise – the best repair is to double-wedge. This is easily achieved by cutting a matched pair of wedges, then gluing and driving them in place at both ends of the tenon.

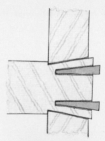

A beautiful double-wedged tenon.

55 **DOWEL LOCATION** A common mistake when assembling a blind dowel joint is marking out and drilling the holes only to find that the dowels are out of alignment. If you don't use commercial dowel centers, a good tip is to sandwich a couple of small ball bearings on a piece of tape. Set the tape in place between the two elements that are to be jointed, and then strike one or other of the components with a mallet. Of course, when you remove the tape, the dowel positions will be perfectly set out on both mating faces.

Dowel centers.

56

BROKEN TENON

Picture this: You have cut and worked all the rails for a piece of furniture, and all the joinery is beautifully cut. Then, right at the last moment, one of the tenons crumbles and disintegrates. What to do? The answer is first to cut the damaged stub of the tenon back to the level of the shoulders. Then scribe the width of the tenon around to the underside of the rail. Saw and pare out the waste so that you are left with an angled bridle slot, and then cut and glue a wedge-tenon stub into the slot. If you have done it right, the mend will only be visible on the underside of the rail.

1. Cut the damage back to the shoulder and make two saw cuts – to match the tenon.

2. Pare out the angled bridle slot.

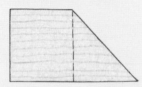

Cut the loose tenon to push-fit in the mortise.

Bridle mortise slot.

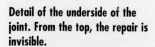

Detail of the underside of the joint. From the top, the repair is invisible.

BASIC LATHE WORK

As most mainstream woodworkers figure that they need know only a little about woodturning – no doubt their thinking being that they are only going to turn the occasional spindle, knob, bun foot, or whatever – it follows that their woodturning activities are loaded with mistakes. The following tips pick up on the seven most common woodturning problems.

57 GOUGE SLIP The situation: The turning is three quarters finished, and you goof up and let the gouge slip. Now there is a great gash in the side of your otherwise beautifully turned spindle. The response is not to rip the workpiece off the lathe and stamp on it. Just cut out the damage with two saw cuts, cut a matched wedge to fit, clean up mating faces, and then glue it in place with super glue (cyanoacrylate glue). Finally, you can trim away the bulk of the patch with a knife and then turn it down to a good finish. It's best if all these procedures are done while the workpiece is still on the lathe.

1. A typical gouge slip goof.

2. The repair is almost invisible.

58 **HIDDEN CAVITY** It often happens in woodturning that the workpiece suddenly reveals an unexpected cavity. A quick fix is to plane the turning down to a level finish, glue and clamp a generous lump of well matched wood to the level face – so that the run of the grain is perfectly aligned – and then turn the repair down to match the profile.

1. Use a small plane to level off the problem area.

2. Glue and clamp a piece of matched wood on the level face and make good.

59 **ALL TAPED UP** A delicate spindle that starts to split at one or both ends while it is being turned, can be rescued. All you do is wind back the tailstock slightly to release the tension, ease as much super glue (cyanoacrylate glue) as you can into the end cracks, strap the ends up with a dozen or so turns of masking tape, and then wind back the tailstock and carry on turning.

60 **BROKEN SPINDLE** If you make the almost routine mistake of snapping off a delicate spindle while it is being turned, the easiest repair is first to cut the spindle back to the nearest bead. Then drill, glue and dowel-fix a new length of wood to the sawn face. Finally, resume turning. If you have done it right, and the joint occurs in a valley or reveal, it will be almost invisible.

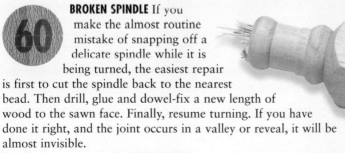

LINE OF MEND

NEW PIECE

DOWEL

BROKEN SPINDLE

Make the mend at the bead line.

61 **STUBBY LEGS** Of all woodturning blunders, designing and making a table, dresser or cupboard that is a bit too short in the legs must surely come high in the "most stupid mistakes" list. That said, the mistake can easily be made good by variously turning a nice set of hardwood cups, or ball feet, or spigotted extensions in a contrasting wood. The secret of success is not to try to hide the additions, but rather to make them a positive feature.

62 **CHUCK REGISTRATION** Although a four-jaw chuck is one of the best ways of ensuring that the workpiece is held secure, if you do need to remove the workpiece for drilling or whatever, then it's not so easy to re-center. Consequently the workpiece is set slightly off-center, and the turning is less than perfect. The problem of misalignment can be prevented simply by numbering the four jaws, and numbering the corresponding four dents on the workpiece made by the jaws before you remove the workpiece.

63 **FOUR-JAW CHUCK** A big mistake when woodturning is to remove the workpiece in the middle of a turning sequence – for drilling on the bench press for example – only to find, when you come back to mounting the workpiece on the lathe, that it is almost impossible to achieve perfect realignment. The best way of putting an end to this particular problem is to get yourself a four-jaw chuck. Then you can move the workpiece and the chuck together.

For swift and easy realignment, number the chuck jaws and the dents on the workpiece.

ASSEMBLING, GLUING, AND CLAMPING

For many woodworkers, the wind-up procedures at the end of a project – of assembling, gluing, and clamping, are at the very heart of the woodworking experience. They somehow or other feel that the real joy and challenge of woodworking is in the tricky-sticky struggle against the woody domain of brute strength, ingenuity, glue and clamps. Maybe they are right. The following tips will help you to fix the most common mistakes.

64 BULGING DRAWERS If you are building a drawer with glued slips under the base – rather than grooves – and you find at the assembly stage that the sides of the drawers bulge or bow, then a quick fix, is to swap the drawer sides over, so that the bow occurs on the inside of the drawer. If you do this, the bowed sides will be pushed apart by the drawer base.

1. Drawer sides bulging outwards.

2. Change the drawer sides over so that they bulge inwards.

3. The drawer base will force the sides into alignment.

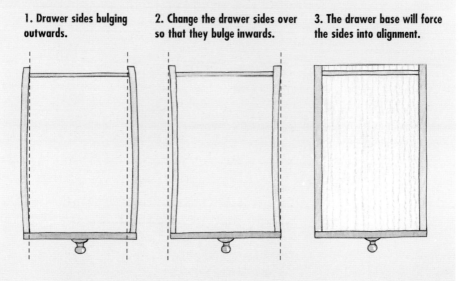

65 GLUE AND SHAVINGS Massive glue squeeze-out is a nuisance in the woodshop and a general all-round mistake. You should use only as much glue as is necessary for good bonding. That means little squeeze-out. But if you do make a big mess, it's a good idea to mop up the excess glue with shavings. For example, if you have glued up a stack of slabs to make a blank for turning a bowl, and you intend clamping the whole works in the jaws of the vise, then you could spread shavings on the floor under the vise to catch the glue ooze.

66 HIDE GLUE A frequent mistake made when using hot hide glue, is to be so generous that the glue collects in the corners and holes. The difficulty is how to remove the hard build-up without swamping the frame in hot water. The answer is to heat up an old chisel and then to hold the chisel on the glue in such a way that when the hot chisel starts to melt the glue, the liquid runs down the shaft.

67 BLOCK PLANE If you find that your last-minute planing and tidying up frequently results in wood splitting off – as when cleaning up the corners of a dovetail joint – chances are you are making the mistake of using a plane that has a high-angled cutter. The recipe for success in this situation is simply to use a block plane. Although this solution might on the face of it seem too easy, the fact is that the design of the block plane – the set of the blade – is such that there is less tendency for the grain to break off. For better results, use a special low-angle block plane, which has the blade set even shallower.

Get yourself a small block plane – the size and low blade angle make it ideal for quality cuts.

68 **NOISY DRAWERS** Fitting drawers is always something of a problem: Either they are too tight, or too loose, or warped across the corners, and so on. If you have a real problem drawer, one that is loose, noisy, a little bit twisted, and with slightly warped sides, you can go a long way to putting it right by simply cutting a bottom that is perfectly square and slightly too tight. What happens is that when the oversized bottom is gently eased into place, it tends to pull the drawer tight and true.

A bench plane with the blade iron bedded at 45 degrees.

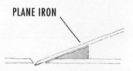

PLANE IRON

A block plane with the blade iron bedded at 20 degrees.

A fine angle block plane with the blade bedded at 12 degrees.

1. Use a strip of paper to ease glue into the offending tear out.

2. Strap up the repair with tape – until the glue is set.

TEAR OUTS
Tear out is one of the commonest and one of the most annoying of all woodworking mistakes. A blade is too dull, or you are trying to hurry a job that won't be rushed, or you twist a saw, and before you can say "stupid-stupid-stupid" one of the component parts is torn. The joyous news is that all such small rips, splits and tears can easily be repaired with super glue (cyanoacrylate glue). Just dribble the glue into the tear, strap up with a clamp or tape, wait a few minutes, and then go back to work. Don't leave the tear to gather dirt, dust and debris – it must be repaired immediately.

70 **DRY-RUN CLAMPING** A frequent woodworking groan-and-moan goes something like, "The project was fine until I came to gluing up." The primary mistakes that most beginners make when they come to gluing are: They try to do everything in a rush; they fail to spread a thin layer of glue on all mating surfaces; and, worst of all, they simply aren't organized. Okay, so there's no denying that you do need to have the correct tools and materials for the job, but that said, you should always have one or more dry-run sessions before you ever touch the glue. It's most important that everything is close at hand, and you know the assembly sequence.

Work out the working area, the type and condition of the clamps, the type of glue, the number of wooden pads – all before you start smearing on the glue.

Pieces of cork floor tile make excellent padding between cramp heads and vulnerable wood.

DRIBBLING GLUE If you are using white or yellow PVA glue and you are so generous with the glue that it runs in a great dribble down the front of your project, on no account be tempted to wipe it off with a cloth. Leave it until the glue becomes rubbery – about 15 minutes to a half hour. Then you can gently peel up the excess with the help of a putty knife. Even if the glue hardens, it's much easier to chisel off a bead of rock hard glue that is sitting on the surface than it is to sand off glue that has been smeared into the pores.

DRY JOINTS If, after you have glued up and removed the clamps, you discover that one or other of the joints is loose and dry, run a small diameter hole down through the joint – in one side and out the other – and inject as much glue as you can into the joint. Finally, while the glue is still runny, drive dowels into the holes, so as to pump the glue into the very heart of the joint.

1. Use a syringe to flood the loose joint with glue.

1. Don't be tempted to wipe the glue off with a cloth.

2. Drive in the dowel to force the glue into all parts of the joint cavity.

2. Wait until the offending glue dribble is transparent and rubbery, then pare it off with a chisel.

FITTINGS, FIXTURES, AND HARDWARE

A great many woodworkers enjoy all the making stages of sawing, planing, joinery and assembly, only to be totally frustrated by the final activities of driving in screws, fitting handles and hinges, attaching knobs, hanging doors and the like. No doubt they are scared off by the notion that one slip-up spells ruin. They know, of course, that many critical design and construction blunders don't come to light until the final stage of assembly. The good news is that you can usually make good with a little ingenuity. The following tips will show you how.

73

SCREW DOWELS A common mistake made by beginners is to butt joint and screw two members to make a right-angled frame only to find that the screws won't hold in the end grain. The problem is, of course, that by the time the joint fails it has usually been covered or built in at back and front. The quick fix is to draw out the screws, drill and dowel at right angles across the line of the screw holes, and then to replace the screws so that they run through the sides of the dowels. For best results, use the largest diameter dowels and smear them with glue before driving them home.

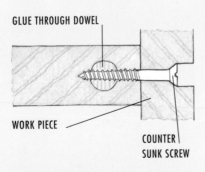

Arrange the dowel so that the screw runs across the grain.

Drive the screw through the joint and on into the dowel.

DEEP-SET HINGE A frequent mistake when installing hinges is to cut the hinge mortises too deep. Then the door either fails to close or threatens to tear the stile. If this is the problem, then insert one or more strips of card or veneer packing to fit the hinge mortise until the door closes to a good tight fit.

A well-set hinge.

Use strips of card to pack out an overly deep hinge mortise.

BIGGER HINGE If you cut a recess too big for your hinge – too long and too wide – sometimes a swift fix is to simply buy a bigger hinge and recut the recess to fit. This time around, don't make the same mistake. Alternatively, patch the recess and start over.

1. A hinge with a badly-cut oversized recess.

2. Select a hinge that is bigger than the goof and then cut a perfect recess the next time around.

3. If you have to use the same hinge, then patch the recess and try for a better fit.

76 **LOOSE KNOBS** A nasty little mistake when making and fitting traditional turned wooden knobs to drawers – meaning knobs with round tenons designed to be glued into holes – is to oversize the hole in the drawer front so the knob tenon is too loose. If this is the case, the simplest solution is to dip the tenon in glue, wind thin twine around the glued tenon until it is a shade too big for the drawer hole, and then push and twist the whole works into place.

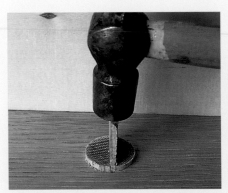

1. Arrange the knob so that the slot runs across the drawer front grain, and tap the glued wedge home.

2. Plane the tenon back flush with the inside face of the drawer.

77 **WEDGED KNOBS** If you have a drawer with oversize knob holes but don't much like the idea of the glue and twine, you can saw a slot in the tenon. Once you set the knob in place, tap a glued wedge into the slot from the inside of the drawer. Once the glue dries, cut the wedge back flush with the drawer. If you think you might want to change the knobs at a later date, then skip the glue and the trimming.

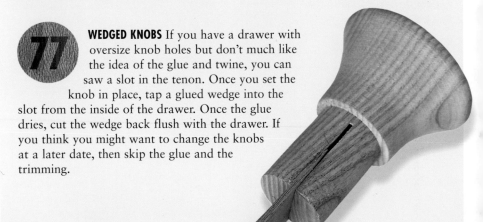

78

WIDER SPADE HOLES If you have to re-drill, for example, a ½-inch diameter hole with a 1-inch spade bit, the difficulty is that the 1-inch bit may wander because it doesn't have anything to center on. The neat answer is to cut a length of dowel to slide nicely into the ½-inch hole, and then center the large-size bit on the plug.

1. Cut a dowel to fit the hole.

2. Center the larger bit on the plug and re-drill.

79

BROKEN SCREWS If you have made the frustrating mistake of twisting the head off a screw – and it's an easy mistake to make if you are using brass screws without pilot holes – don't despair. All you do is cut a short length of the smallest possible diameter steel tube that will fit over the screw. Then file a few cuts across one end of the tube, and use the tube like a miniature hole saw to run a drilled hole down around the screw. This done, you can twist out the core with the broken screw, glue and plug the hole with matching wood, and then re-screw – but this time drill a pilot hole for the screw.

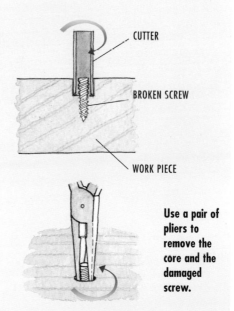

CUTTER

BROKEN SCREW

WORK PIECE

Use a pair of pliers to remove the core and the damaged screw.

VENEERS AND INLAY

O ver the last few years, there has been a tremendous resurgence of interest in veneering and inlaying. Gone are the days when veneering was only about hot glues, hammers, plywood, and cauls. Now at last, with the introduction of modern adhesives and the interest in stable sheet materials like medium-density fiberboard (MDF), woodworkers are once again experimenting with all manner of colored veneers and inlays. The bad news is that many new woodworkers are coming to grief and making mistakes. The good news is that the following tips will help put matters right.

80 **VENEER MITER** Thin veneers are a great way of covering up mistakes. Let's say that you have made a picture frame with four horrible miters, and the design is such that a ¹⁄₁₆ inch thickness isn't going to be noticed. All you do is cut four strips of veneer and cross them over at the corner. Then run a steel rule across the intersection and use a sharp knife to cut through both strips at once. Remove the waste and then stick down as described in the following tips.

1. Arrange the two strips so that they intersect at right angles.

2. Slice across the diagonal.

81

BLISTERING VENEER It sometimes happens that a small air pocket gets trapped under veneer, with the effect that there is a bump or blister. The best way to solve this problem is to first use a scalpel to slit the blister along the line of the grain. If you have used PVA or hide glue, you can reglue with a hot iron. If, however, the veneer was originally stuck down with urea-formaldehyde glue, then squeeze superglue (cyanoacrylate glue) into the slit and apply pressure with a waxed block.

1. Carefully slit the blister along the line of the grain.

2. Use a sliver of paper to introduce thermo-reactive glue into the heart of the blister.

3. Use a hot iron to make good.

82

EDGE TEAR-UP You have veneered a panel, say the side of a cabinet, and you make a clumsy move that results in the edge getting torn. The quick fix is to first take a piece of nicely matched veneer and tape it in place over the damaged area so that the grain is aligned. Then cut through the double layer and down to the base board or substrate. Use a sharp chisel to pare the substrate to a smooth finish. Next apply coated cement and set in the veneer patch.

Cut through the double layer to achieve a perfectly sized patch.

83 **LIFT AND PATCH** A nasty problem that occasionally crops up when veneering, is that a loose knot in the groundwork crumbles and rises, with the effect that there is a solid bump under the veneer. If this happens, you have to either scrap the whole job or lift and repair. The remedy is to cut a patch as already described – one that is larger than the bump. Then use the chisel to cut out the damaged substrate and to make a diamond-shaped recess. Glue and plug the recess. When the glue is dry, trim the plug down to a good finish, and finally fit the veneer patch with contact cement.

84 **TOTAL LIFT** A frequent mistake made by beginners who use heat-activated glues is that they overheat and overwork the veneer to the point that it needs to be lifted and re-attached. If this is the case, the safest procedure is to cover the whole sheet of veneer with edge-to-edge strips of masking tape, and then carefully ease the whole layer up with a hot iron and hot scraper. You will need help – one person to be ironing and lifting, and the other person to be working the warm scraper underneath the veneer. When you come to re-attach the veneer, start from one side, all the while making sure that the glue is melting, and that stuck-down areas are free from air pockets.

85 **PANEL WARP** A mistake made by penny-pinching beginners to veneering is that they veneer only one side of the work. Because the veneered side reacts differently to seasonal changes in moisture and humidity, and especially if the substrate is a thin board, then it usually warps. If this happens, the quick fix is to balance the stress by veneering the other side of the board. Suppliers sell inexpensive veneers for this purpose.

Mahogany is commonly used for balancing.

Pine - a more sustainable species - is also suitable for balancing.

1. Reinforce the problem veneer with straps of masking tape running across the grain.

2. Melt the glue while a friend gently eases and lifts the veneer.

86 **CRACKS AND HOLLOWS** If, after you have completed a piece of marquetry or parquetry, you find that there are little hollows between neighboring veneers, then the chances are that you have made the mistake of using a water-based contact adhesive. If this is the case, you can fill the cracks with a mix of veneer sawdust and common white or yellow PVA glue.

Fill the fault with a mix of sawdust and PVA glue, and rub down to a good finish.

EDGE LIFT Beginners often over-clamp and/or over-sand the edges of veneered work, with the result that the edge lifts and is at risk. If this is your problem, set the tabletop or other veneered workpiece on its edge on a pad of scrap carpet so that the edge lift is looking to the sky. Then use the blade of a scalpel to work as much PVA glue as possible down between the veneer and the substrate. When you are sure that glue has run deeply into the pocket, wipe away excess, and clamp up with blocks and c-clamps. Be sure to place wax paper between the blocks and the workpiece.

1. Use a scalpel and sliver of paper to ease glue down into the cavity.

2. Wet wax paper between the workpiece and the blocks, and then clamp.

CUTS AND SCRATCHES If you slip with your knife to the extent that some small part of the veneer is scratched across the grain, you will be left with a mark that needs attention before it fills up with dirt and dust. The remedy is to first dribble a few drops of water on the cut. Then take the finest scalpel and scratch in line with the grain and across the cut. Do this on both sides of the cut so as to raise and fluff up the grain and conceal the damage.

1. What a mistake to make!

2. Dampen the scratch and gently tease the fibers with the point of the scalpel.

3. Tease in the direction of the grain until the scratch vanishes from view.

WARPED STOCK
What do you do if you have spent good money on a piece of expensive veneer only to find that it starts to warp and buckle? The answer is having first repeatedly dampened pressed and dried the veneer – between boards and under weights – brush the "glue" face of the veneer with wallpaper sizing, sandwich it between sheets of wax paper, and press it under weighted boards until it is dry. This will usually leave the veneer as flat as a pancake and ready to use.

1. Saturate the warped veneer with water and brush on a coat of size – on the face to be glued.

2. Set the veneer between sheets of wax paper.

3. Sandwich the whole works between boards and press with a heavy weight.

Burr walnut

Figured maple

FINISHING, ASSEMBLY, AND SHOWING

Of all the woodworking stages, the culmination of assembly, laying on coats of varnish and oil, and generally adjusting everything to a fine fit and finish is both the most exciting and the most nerve wracking. At last the project is finished and on show – the character of the wood, your designing and construction skills – everything is on view. And of course, as you are exhausted and excited, this is where you are going to make some really basic goofs. But not to worry, just take it nice and easy, and stay with the following tips.

 FALLING FORWARD If you have made the classic mistake of designing and building a tall cabinet or bookcase that falls forward when the upper doors are opened, a good tip is to take a shaving or two off the bottom back edge. Then the whole piece will lean slightly back against the wall.

 FUZZY GRAIN Some woods are a real pest to bring to a good smooth finish. No matter how hard you try, the grain raises and generally goes fuzzy. The best procedure for achieving a smooth finish is to lay on a glue sizing mix to seal the surface and raise the grain. Let it dry before using a cabinet scraper to skim off the raised grain. Resist the temptation to use sandpaper – a scraper does the job better.

1. Brush size on the fuzzy surface and leave it to dry.

2. Use a scraper to cut the grain nibs down to a good finish.

BLOOMING BLUSH If you have made the mistake of brushing on varnish or lacquer on a day when the humidity is too high, your workpiece may develop a worrisome condition known as blush or bloom. The varnish will look white and cloudy. The secret is not to panic, but rather to wait a day or two and see what happens. If you are lucky the blush will disappear of its own accord. If you are not so lucky, give the workpiece a swift sanding with the finest garnet paper and lay on another thin coat of varnish or lacquer. Follow the finish manufacturer's recommendations for temperature and humidity during application.

A classic example of varnish bloom.

BURN-IN STICKS Wax filler sticks called burn-in sticks are a bit like kids' wax crayons. They are a great quick-fix product for filling in all those dents and scratches that sometimes happen when the piece of furniture is transported. For very minor repairs, you just choose a color to match your finish, then rub the wax stick into the small scratch or hole, and finally polish the repair to a good finish. If the hole is more than about ⅛ inch deep, best apply the burn-in stick according to the manufacturer's directions, with a hot knife.

1. Use a hot knife or soldering iron to puddle the offending dent with colored wax.

2. Rub the repair down with fine grade garnet paper.

3. Continue rubbing down until you achieve a good finish.

94 **DENTED VARNISH** Although at first sight a dent in beautiful clear varnish finish can look to be a huge mistake, it can easily be removed by adding more coats of the same varnish. All you do is touch in a dab of varnish and let it dry, then touch in another dab and let it dry, and so on and on, until the dent has been topped up. Don't be tempted to fill the dent by pouring the varnish – if you do, it will pucker.

1. Dab a small amount of varnish into the dent.

2. Repeat until the dent has been topped up.

3. Rub the dry varnish down with fine grade garnet paper.

95 **BURN MARKS** Though a cigarette burn is one of those really annoying mistakes that shouldn't be allowed to happen, the truth is that cigarette burns are a common woodshop blunder. The simple repair is not to try to remove the burn mark with sandpaper, but rather to scrape the burn out with a cabinet scraper. Run the scraper diagonally across the grain – first one way and then the other – and then finish up by scraping parallel to the grain.

1. Run the scraper diagonally across the grain.

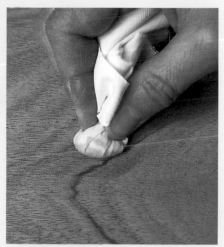

4. Use metal polish to cut the repair down to polished finish.

VARNISH BUBBLES

96 Although you can't do much about bubbles that have dried in a coat of varnish – other than to scrape off the varnish and start over – you can make sure that you don't make the same mistake the next time around. The best procedure is only to brush on thin coats, and to always let one coat dry before you attempt to apply another.

Scrape the varnish off and start over.

2. Work the whole area – this way and that – until the burn mark has been cut back.

1. A surface that shows signs of spots and smears of glue.

GLUE SPOTS Glue spots left on the surface are a big mistake. When the surface comes to be oiled, waxed or otherwise finished, the spots suddenly reveal themselves as flaws in the finish. The fail-safe procedure before finishing is to first highlight spots by rubbing the whole surface down with mineral spirits, then to remove the spots with a cabinet scraper before applying the finish.

2. Highlight the spots by brushing with mineral spirits.

3. Rub down with garnet paper prior to applying the finish.

DUST FREE If you make the mistake of wiping on tung oil and the like with a lint-covered cloth, then you will almost certainly finish up with a surface that is dusty and generally less than perfect. If you want to side-step this mistake, then be sure to use wipes made from old cotton sheets or wipes made from non-woven type tissues. That said, if you do make a mess-up, then use a lint-free cloth and mineral spirits or naptha to clean up before re-oiling.

99 **WATER SPOTS** Being mindful that water spots are likely to spoil a finish, you should do your best to avoid them in the first place. If, however, a board gets rained on or whatever, the best quick-fix is to wash the whole board, then at least any subsequent difficulties will be uniform.

1. Water spots might well spoil the finish.

2. Brush water over the entire surface to achieve uniformity.

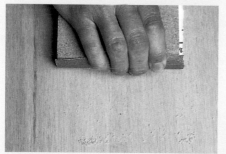

3. Rub the dry wood over with garnet paper.

100 **SPARE PARTS** One of the horrors of woodwork – a huge mistake in fact – has to do with putting a project together, only to find that one or other of the small, fragile, difficult-to-make parts is broken, or is missing, or has been chewed by the dog, or whatever. The wonderfully simple answer to this problem is to always make a spare. For example, you could make five bun feet on the lathe rather than four, or you could cut out three chair splats rather than two, and so on.

CREDITS

Quarto Publishing would like to acknowledge and thank the following who loaned tools and equipment featured in this book.

Axminster Power Tool Centre, Chard Street, Axminster, Devon (Tools and equipment)

D. & J. Simon and Sons, 122–125 Hackney Road, London EC2 (Wooden spindles)

J. Crispin and Sons, 94 Curtain Road, London EC2 (Veneers)

We would also like to thank Tim Hodgkinson, Simone Oliver and Alan Thomas at Pendryn Furniture, 2b Barbican Industrial Estate, East Looe, Cornwall, who kindly permitted us to photograph at their premises.

Finally, our thanks to Hescot Ltd, Newmarket, Suffolk, who allowed us to reproduce the Michael Thonet chair on page 8.

Senior Art editor Penny Cobb
Designer Glyn Bridgewater
Photographers Ian Howes, Jeremy Thomas
Illustrator Gill Bridgewater
Text editor William Sampson
Senior editor Kate Kirby
Prop researcher Miriam Hyman
Picture manager Giulia Hetherington
Editorial director Mark Dartford
Art director Moira Clinch

Typeset by Central Southern Typesetters, Eastbourne
Manufactured by Bright Arts (Singapore) Pte Ltd.
Printed in China by Leefung-Asco Printers Ltd.